Ground cover plants

Cover: like many other cranesbills, *Geranium psilostemon* is a
decorative and easily grown ground cover
Overleaf: the attractive evergreen leaves of *Epimedium perralderianum*
set off the flowers in early spring

Ground cover plants

A Wisley handbook

Cassell

The Royal Horticultural Society

Cassell Educational Limited
Artillery House, Artillery Row
London SW1P 1RT
for the Royal Horticultural Society

First published 1975
Second edition 1985
Third edition, fully revised and reset 1989

British Library Cataloguing in Publication Data
Ground cover plants
  1. Ground cover plants
  Royal Horticultural Society
  635.9′64

ISBN 0–304–31089–1

Photographs by Michael Warren
Design by Lesley Stewart

Phototypesetting by Chapterhouse, Formby
Printed in Hong Kong by Wing King Tong Co. Ltd

Contents

Introduction

Ground cover is a term that has been used often in the horticultural literature of the last thirty years. It is a technique of growing plants close together so that they make a continuous canopy of leaves over the soil. This canopy must be thick enough to prevent any other plants (i.e. weeds) from becoming established below it. The weeds will not thrive chiefly because of lack of light, but also because of root competition for water and nutrients. This situation is natural in the wild, where plants most suited to a particular environment will survive, flourish and smother the weaker plants. The difference in the garden is that the gardener, not the environment, chooses what is to grow and survive.

A garden is an artificial environment. Almost all our garden plants have been either introduced from other climates or bred for characters that would not necessarily allow them to survive in the wild in this country. All cultivation of garden plants is directed at creating and maintaining an artificial population. But in doing this it is sensible to adopt natural methods, as in the ground cover approach.

The theory of ground cover, therefore, is to use ornamental plants to cover areas of soil in the garden so thickly that no weeds can compete. In the modern interpretation the plants used must be those that can thrive with only minimum maintenance. Neither grass nor carpet bedding qualify, because although they fulfil the first requirement they need a lot of labour – grass must be regularly mowed to keep it looking controlled, and carpet bedding needs even more work in the annual production of new plants. The types of plant which do qualify are perennial and hardy for the area where they are to grow.

Although the technique is not really a new one, it is particularly applicable to modern gardens with little available labour, and where there are fairly large areas which can sensibly and attractively be devoted to ground cover plants. In general, appropriate plants are relatively low and spreading; those with upright, open-branched growth are unsuitable as they do not exclude light from the soil surface and allow weeds to flourish. There is no clear

Opposite: the lesser periwinkle, *Vinca minor*, and its forms are some of the most efficient ground covers

7

Stachys olympica 'Silver Carpet' lives up to its name in a sunny position

dividing line between plants that are good as ground cover and those that are not. In between come many plants whose effectiveness as ground cover depends on the gardener and on the environment. Choosing suitable plants for the conditions and encouraging them to grow well are important factors for success with ground cover.

Some enthusiasts give the impression that almost all members of the plant kingdom can be used as ground cover. In practice, only a proportion are satisfactory. When starting with ground cover in the garden, it is better to choose easily controlled and easily cultivated plants and a selection is given on pp.24–60. All have their disadvantages as well as advantages. Either they are easy to establish and will continue growing vigorously so that later they need to be restrained, or they need a good deal of attention to get them to flourish. Some start off well and are excellent for a year or two but then gradually deteriorate. Be prepared for some degree of compromise, according to the situation and conditions of the individual garden.

Why use ground cover?

The main reason for using ground cover is to reduce the time spent on keeping the ground clear of weeds between the desirable plants. The effect of a complete carpet of plants also gives an attractive natural appearance.

Most people will still want some area of lawn in the garden, for sitting out, and no other ground cover has such tolerance to human traffic. But there are many places where ground cover can be recommended instead of grass. In shade, for instance, grass will rarely grow well, whereas numerous ground cover plants will thrive. Shade beneath trees is particularly difficult, partly because of competing roots and partly because the light conditions beneath a tree will change as the tree grows, and so after a few years the plants chosen initially for light shade may need to be replaced by others that will tolerate denser shade. (See also the Wisley handbook, *Plants for Shade*.)

The purple-leaved *Viola labradorica* and the foam flower, *Tiarella cordifolia*, thrive in shade

Grass banks are another problem garden feature, being both awkward and often dangerous to mow. An alternative is to plant permanent ground cover, which may also help to stabilize the bank and prevent soil erosion.

Shrub (including rose) borders too can be planted with lower ground cover plants to give a pleasing community of varying heights. There is one snag that may arise and that is to keep the shrubs sufficiently well fed. With such a dense community of competing plants, regular feeding is essential. Foliar nutrition may also be useful (see p.22).

Ground cover plants can be used almost anywhere in the garden – to edge beds and borders, in a rock garden and over large areas which might otherwise be time-consuming to maintain. Often we achieve 'ground cover' without realising it, but to be effective it usually requires careful planning, together with the right selection of plants for the aspect and soil.

The rose of Sharon, *Hypericum calycinum*, has become naturalised in parts of Britain

What can be used?

Plants suitable for ground cover are by definition perennials, that is, shrubs or herbaceous plants. Annuals and biennials are too short-lived to compete with weeds, although there may sometimes be a place for a spreading low-growing annual such as *Limnanthes douglasii* as a 'filler' in the first year between the permanent perennials.

Almost any plant which has a spreading habit of growth is in its way acting as ground cover. Although many plants are recommended, it is as well to realise that a considerable number – hellebores, pulsatillas, *Claytonia sibirica* and various rock plants like *Acantholimon* among them – which are sometimes suggested, do not really fulfil the function of ground cover as defined here, either because the foliage canopy they make is not dense enough to suppress the weeds effectively, or because it is very slow to cover the ground.

The main requirements of a good ground cover plant are:

(a) Hardiness, in an average winter, in the area concerned. As an example, *Hypericum calycinum* is usually hardy throughout Britain. *Osteospermum* (*Dimorphotheca*) 'Nairobi Purple', although an excellent ground cover, is less likely to survive the winter at the RHS Garden, Wisley, than in Cornwall where winters are usually less severe.

(b) Tolerance of other adverse conditions, particularly periods of drought or extended wet weather.

(c) Sufficient vigour to cover the available ground in the first or second season after planting.

(d) The ability to form a dense, relatively low-growing cover and to remain in good condition for a number of years (at least 5 to 10) without requiring very much attention. Evergreens may be more effective in fulfilling this requirement, as deciduous plants, such as hostas, allow annual weeds (chickweed, cleavers, and grass) to grow after the foliage has died down and particularly in early spring before their leaves have developed fully to cover the ground again.

(e) A degree of beauty and interest as a garden plant during the year. Attractive flowers and/or fruits at some season, or foliage which is interesting in shape, pattern, texture or colour are very desirable. Good foliage, particularly of evergreens, which will be seen by the gardener throughout the

11

The hummock-forming *Ceanothus thyrsiflorus* var. *repens* is a hardy and attractive evergreen shrub

year, is most important.

(f) Low maintenance. An annual feeding or top-dressing and a clip-over or removal of dying foliage are all that should be needed. The plant should also be more or less free of the usual pests and diseases – spraying is work and costs money. Some evergreen ground covers (and also deciduous plants like hostas) in damp conditions are havens for slugs and snails, which will require control.

There is a wide range of plants, both woody and herbaceous, which fulfil these requirements. However, the particular garden conditions in which the plants are to be grown should also be considered and the gardener must make the best of the situation and the plants available.

Garden conditions

Every garden is different, in soil, in climate, and in man-made features such as walls and their effect on the environment. These conditions can be altered to some extent, but a less laborious way of gardening is to choose plants that will grow well in the existing conditions, or with some relatively minor amendments to them.

First, these conditions must be analysed. In a small garden there will be quite a variation in the microclimate, even in the course of one day. One part has morning sun, one has evening sun, another has sun all day, or no sun at all. Combine these variations with those of rainfall, frost, wind during the year, and soil, and it is clear that plants must be able to adapt to a range of conditions.

Rainfall cannot be controlled but can be supplemented if necessary by watering. The amount of sunshine in a particular position can be exploited by using plants that like the sun or those that grow best in the shade. Similarly, wind-tolerant plants can be chosen for very exposed gardens. Frost should only be a problem in exceptional years if hardy plants are grown.

Soils can be improved, although it takes time. The ideal soil for most plants is a neutral loam, neither too light in texture (sand) nor too heavy (clay). There are few ideal soils, but much can be done to improve soil texture, primarily by adding humus (see p.18). Any type of humus can be used; garden compost, farmyard manure, leafmould, pulverised bark, mushroom compost (which is often alkaline), and peat are among suitable types most often available.

Less can be done to alter soil alkalinity or acidity, and it is a long-term process, so it is simpler to choose plants that are suited to the existing soil conditions – ericas, for example, on acid soils.

'Annemarie', one of the numerous cultivars of *Calluna vulgaris*

Above: the distinctive foliage of *Hosta undulata* var. *univittata* with a broad cream stripe in the centre
Below: 'Coral Beauty', a recently introduced form of the carpeting *Cotoneaster dammeri*

Types of ground cover plants

There are two main groups of herbaceous ground covers – clump-formers; and carpeters or colonisers. The first are relatively slow and steady growers, the second are fast growing but may in some instances produce a thinner canopy. Under 'herbaceous' are included bergenias and some epimediums, which keep their leaves over the winter, and therefore are not strictly herbaceous.

Shrubs too can be grouped in broadly the same way – those that produce a dense network of branches to form hummocks over several years; and those which spread more rapidly by rooting into the soil as they travel, or by producing suckers from underground roots.

For the purposes of this book, ground cover plants have been divided into six groups according to the type of cover they make. These divisions are arbitrary, and some overlap is inevitable.

A. Quick growing evergreens with dense twiggy growth, either carpeters or colonisers. These are the most efficient ground covers, and will make an almost complete canopy in the first year after planting at the distances recommended. Examples are certain cultivars of ivy, *Hedera helix*, and forms of the lesser periwinkle, *Vinca minor*.

B. Evergreens of dense growth which will take two seasons to cover the ground completely at the distances recommended. Alternatively, but more expensively, they can be planted closer together to obtain a good canopy in the first year. They may need extra encouragement, such as pruning, to stimulate more branching near the soil surface. *Erica herbacea* (*E.carnea*), dwarf junipers and *Alyssum* (*Aurinia*) *saxatilis* are examples of these hummock-forming or slow carpeting or colonising plants.

C. Deciduous clump-forming plants, which make thick cover with their leaves during the growing season, but die down during winter. Although there is no cover at that time their dense network of roots competes to some extent with annual weeds that may try to grow in the winter; but they are not completely effective ground covers and early spring weeding to remove weeds such as chickweed and annual meadow grass is often necessary. These are the slow but steady herbaceous type; examples are *Hemerocallis* (daylilies), hostas, *Alchemilla mollis* and geraniums such as *G. wallichianum* which, although wide spreading, does not (or very rarely) root at the nodes.

D. Carpeters or colonisers, deciduous or evergreen, which either make a network of stems over the ground, rooting into the soil as they travel, or send out stolons or sucker growths, often from their roots. These often cover the soil area rapidly, but not all make such a dense cover as groups A to C, even in summer. Eventually they form thick mats of growth but during the first season before cover is complete they are likely to need regular weeding. Examples are Duchesnea (Fragaria) indica, Glechoma hederacea 'Variegata' and acaenas.

E. Trailers which do not generally branch and root so much but have an 'umbrella-spoke' habit; they may be deciduous or evergreen. Because of their long growths these plants take longer than the earlier groups to make a thick cover and the gardener needs to have patience. Examples are Rosa 'Max Graf' and Clematis. They have the considerable drawback of requiring at least two years of weed control and this is not always easy to carry out. In some situations, particularly on banks, they have their uses, but it is essential to deal with the weeds initially if they are to be successful.

F. A last group may be mentioned, but with reservations. It consists of plants which are often so vigorous that unless regularly restrained they may swamp their neighbours. Such plants can sometimes be more trouble than they are worth, because of the amount of attention they need. Among them we include the various climbers sometimes suggested (e.g. the honeysuckles, Lonicera japonica halliana and L. henryi) which make a good canopy, but need considerable and regular control, unless they are planted in areas where they have room to spread without strangling their neighbours.

The aim of this book is to guide gardeners to plants that will be effective without constantly needing long-term attention and the list on pp.24–60 contains a selection of the most satisfactory and reliable plants for the purpose.

Preparing and planting

To grow any plant successfully a favourable environment needs to be created and maintained. Almost all garden plants are incomers, expected to grow in an unaccustomed climate and to compete with the natives, which are well adapted to the environment. The chosen plants need all the help they can get from the gardener to become established and to flourish.

Having decided where the plants are to grow, the next requirements are to provide a soil bed in good condition for plant growth, and to remove all competitors, i.e. weeds. It is particularly important to eliminate perennial weeds before planting because afterwards it is almost impossible to get out the deep-rooting and persistent weeds without disturbing the other plants.

CONTROL OF ANNUAL WEEDS

Annual weeds are a relatively straightforward problem as they are mostly shallow-rooting and can be easily removed when forking over the soil before planting. With sensible precautions it is also possible to use certain herbicides to prevent the germination of weed seeds in the areas between the freshly planted ground cover and to eliminate seedlings of annual weeds.

Once ground cover plants are well established they should provide a cover sufficiently dense to inhibit or prevent germination of weed seeds, but weed control may be necessary in the first season or two after planting.

CONTROL OF PERENNIAL WEEDS

It cannot be overemphasised that it is essential to remove all perennial weeds before planting any areas of ground cover. Perennial weeds such as ground elder, couch grass and bindweed will compete with ground cover and are almost impossible to control once ground cover has been planted. Where the ground is infested with such persistent weeds, there should be no plans for planting until they have been completely removed.

Both mechanical and chemical methods can be used to remove perennial weeds. Allow a reasonable interval between treatment and planting so that if the weeds have not been completely eliminated there is an opportunity to see and treat any regrowth. By mechanical methods is meant weed removal by hand, by hoe,

17

spade or machine. The last is only feasible before planting; the second and third are not recommended after planting, and the first can be done at any time.

Chemical herbicides must always be used very carefully, and at the correct time of year. Glyphosate is particularly useful against difficult perennial weeds, applied between July and September. Care must be taken that it does not come in contact with cultivated plants. (For further information see the Wisley handbook, *Weed control in the garden*.)

PREPARATION OF THE SOIL

Many people believe that ground cover plants will grow without any particular care in soil preparation. This is a fallacy and may account for the poor results obtained with ground cover in some cases. Proper preparation of the soil is just as important for ground cover plants, if they are to grow well and remain in good condition for some years, as it is for roses.

A soil which is naturally fertile and of good structure is exceptional and most soils will benefit considerably from the incorporation of humus of some type in the top soil layer. The humus is dug in to a spade's depth, preferably in autumn, and the surface is left in a rough condition to weather over the winter.

Humus will improve most soil types, especially if applied regularly, increasing the water-holding capacity of light soils, improving the drainage of heavier soils and providing some of the main nutrients for the plants. But nutrients are present in humus in only relatively small amounts (and hardly at all in most peats) and become available only slowly. An extra supply of nutrients will help plants to become established more quickly, and a general balanced fertilizer, such as Growmore, can be applied before planting, at a rate of 1 to 2 oz per square yard (33 to 66 g per m²).

PLANTING

Now that plants are available in containers at all times of year, they can be planted at any season, but they must be cared for after planting, particularly in hot and dry weather, to make sure that they do not suffer from lack of water. The best time for planting is late autumn, or better still, early spring, when the soil is starting to warm up and usually contains plenty of moisture, which will soon encourage the roots to grow.

The method is the same for all plants. Dig a hole wide enough to take the roots without cramping them and deep enough to take the roots or the soil ball, so that the newly planted plant is at the same

Ground cover plants may look sparse at first, as with *Helianthemum nummularium* 'Amy Baring' (above), but the aim should be to achieve a dense effect such as that of *Hebe rakaiensis* (below)

level in the border as it was in the nursery or container. With container plants it is easy to see that they are neither too deep nor too high; the soil level in the container is the guide. With bare-root shrubs there will be a mark on the stem showing the level of the soil in the nursery before lifting, and the soil after planting in the new position should come to the same level. With bare-root herbaceous plants, the collar of the plant, where roots and shoots join, should be at soil level. When planting bare-root plants do not allow the roots to dry out while they are waiting to be put in – sun and spring winds can sometimes dry out fibrous roots very quickly, so cover the roots with some sheeting or sacking.

When the plant is in the right position, replace the soil and firm it in well all round, finally forking over the surface to make it look tidy.

Spacing at the planting stage depends on the following factors:

1. Type of ground cover (see p.15) i.e. how quickly the plants will cover a given area.
2. Ultimate spread of the plants. This is influenced to some extent by the environmental conditions, e.g. the fertility of the soil.
3. Size of the plants at planting. (See also the list, pp.24–60, for recommended planting distances.)

All these factors need to be correlated to determine the spacing, for the sooner the neighbouring plants meet, the better for weed control. Smaller, younger plants tend to grow more rapidly than larger, older plants because of their greater vigour. But the size of the plants and their cost do also have a bearing on the spacing and eventual coverage. Eight small plants spaced at 18 inches (45 cm) apart may cover the same area more efficiently in the first season than six large plants, planted 3 feet (0.9 m) apart. However, when planting a larger area it may be too expensive to plant for the optimum effect as soon as possible, and so the plants are put in at wider spacing, with the commitment to continue weeding for two seasons instead of one.

Many nursery catalogues give an indication of the spread of the plants, and if buying from a reliable garden centre there should be someone who can guide the buyer on this. It is a good idea to see the plants growing in other people's gardens, or to visit a ground cover demonstration plot such as those at the RHS Garden at Wisley in Surrey, at Probus, near Bodmin, Cornwall, and at the Royal Botanic Garden in Edinburgh.

Maintenance

WEED CONTROL

Once the plants are in, the weed control programme needs to be started and continued regularly, either by hoeing, by herbicides (see p.18), by interplanting (e.g. with annuals) or by mulching. In the first year after planting it is vital to give consistent weed control so that any competition for nutrients and water by other plants is kept to a minimum.

For annual weeds, hoeing or removal by hand as soon as they are seen is the most effective method. If this is done regularly as the seedlings germinate then there should be no problem. Any persistent perennial weeds, such as dandelions and nettles, which may have escaped the initial clearance can be treated with a weedkiller like glyphosate.

MULCHING

A layer 2 to 3 inches (5–7.5 cm) thick of mulching material placed between the freshly planted ground cover is an excellent method of suppressing weed growth and it is beneficial in encouraging the rapid development of the plants. It is important to ensure that the mulch is not contaminated with weed seeds (often a problem with home-made compost) and to remember that many types of mulch are excellent seed beds for wind-blown seeds. But it may be a consolation that the seedlings that do germinate in a good mulch often grow so lushly that they are easy to pluck out. Peat and pulverised bark and any of the materials mentioned on p.13 may be used for mulching. Black polythene is also an effective mulching material.

It is important that the mulch goes between the plants and not on top of the growing shoots of the herbaceous plants which may be smothered themselves. Regular mulching in spring between the clump-formers until they meet will help weed control and also improve the humus content of the soil. Once they have spread into each other it is difficult to get the mulch beneath the plants and on to the soil. A thick layer of mulching material should not be put on top of carpeters or colonisers because it would smother them, but a thinner layer sprinkled between the stems each year in spring will help to keep some humus supplied to the soil.

Woodland plants such as *Pulmonaria angustifolia* benefit particularly from a mulch

FERTILIZING

Fertilizers are not often applied to ground cover in gardens but they should be and will improve growth, and keep it vigorous. Early spring is the time to apply most fertilizers, either a general artificial fertilizer such as Growmore or an organic fertilizer such as bone meal. Slow-release fertilizers can also be very useful. They are more expensive than other fertilizers, but are formulated to release nutrients into the soil over a much longer period. Apply the fertilizer carefully to the soil around the plants in spring, taking care to avoid the foliage as some artificial fertilizers may scorch the leaves.

Foliar feeding is sometimes recommended for plants. This is the application of a diluted liquid feed by spraying on to the leaves which quickly take in the nutrients. Foliar feeding will produce a rapid response from the plant, if applied at the right time, and quickly stimulates plant growth. The most effective times to apply foliar feeds are in late spring and early summer, when extension growth is normally being produced.

The main value of foliar feeding is to reinvigorate and feed plants that are backward in growth, such as those with a poor root

The questing roots of *Hemerocallis fulva* will colonise large areas, but other daylilies form more manageable clumps

system (perhaps due to drought) or those that are not yet established. It can also be useful as a quick feed for shrubs in a border thickly planted with ground cover. However, healthy well-grown plants should not normally need such a life-saving technique.

PRUNING AND DIVISION

Keeping the plants tidy is an occasional job which will be needed for certain plants – those that are very vigorous and have to be restrained from swamping other plants, and those that become straggly after several years and require cutting back to keep them compact, such as ericas. The removal of dead twigs and old flowering stems is also part of regular pruning. With some woody plants pruning may be necessary in the early years after planting to encourage branching near ground level. (See also the Wisley handbook, *Pruning ornamental shrubs*.)

Herbaceous plants like *Alchemilla mollis*, hostas and daylilies may become overcrowded and should be divided after about four to five years.

23

A selection of plants

This chapter contains information on plants suitable for ground cover. These are divided into the four main categories outlined on pp.15–16 and are listed alphabetically by their botanical name within each group.

In most cases, the name of the species or hybrid group is used for the heading, and its approximate height and the planting distance are given at the end of each entry. The height is that of the plant when not in flower; the planting distance is that recommended in order to obtain 75 to 100 per cent cover within one to two years. Both may vary to some extent according to the climate, soil and other factors. Details of soil, aspect or any special requirements are included and varieties, cultivars or similar species are also mentioned where appropriate. The plant is described as deciduous or evergreen according to whether it loses or keeps its leaves in winter.

GROUP A

Evergreens of rapid growth and high density cover which either carpet the ground with spreading stems, rooting as they go, or colonise by means of underground shoots, suckers, or stolons. The most efficient ground covers, making a complete canopy in the first year after planting. All are very tolerant of shade and undemanding in their soil requirements.

Galeobdolon

G. argentatum (Lamium galeobdolon 'Variegatum'), yellow archangel. Perennial carpeter of tremendous vigour with marbled green and white foliage and yellow flowers in early summer. Excellent under trees and shrubs, but avoid areas where small plants might be smothered. Height 6–9 in. (15–23 cm). Planting distance 24–36 in. (60–90 cm).

Hedera (ivy)

Carpeting or climbing shrubs for almost any situation from dense shade to full sun.
H. canariensis 'Azorica'. Large matt-green leaves. 'Gloire de Marengo' ('Variegata') has foliage marked white, grey and green

The robust Irish ivy, *Hedera helix* 'Hibernica', is especially useful beneath trees, where not even grass would grow, and thrives in almost any conditions

but is less reliable in cold gardens. Height 6–9 in. (15–23 cm). Planting distance 36–48 in. (90–120 cm).

H. colchica. Thick dark green leaves. 'Dentata' has paler larger leaves. 'Dentata Variegata' has foliage margined creamy yellow. 'Sulphur Heart' ('Paddy's Pride') has a central splash of gold on the leaves. Height 6–9 in. (15–23 cm). Planting distance 36–48 in. (90–120 cm).

H. helix, common ivy. Extremely variable and adaptable, first-class ground cover. 'Hibernica', Irish ivy, with large dark green leaves, is particularly vigorous, dense and fast-growing. Many other forms, with green or variegated foliage, are suitable, including 'Green Ripple' and 'Goldheart'. Height 6—12 in. (15–30 cm). Planting distance, depending on vigour, 24–48 in. (60–120 cm).

Hypericum (see also p.34)

H. calycinum, rose of Sharon. Colonising shrub with saucer-shaped golden yellow flowers from summer into autumn. Sun or shade in any well-drained soil. Cut to near ground level each April for densest cover. Height 9–12 in. (23–30 cm). Planting distance 15–18 in. (38–46 cm). (See p.10.)

Waldsteinia ternata makes a pretty evergreen carpet in sun or shade, bearing golden yellow flowers in April and May

Vinca (periwinkle)

Carpeting, trailing shrubs.
V. *major*. Blue or white flowers in spring. Ideal for almost any position and soil, except poorly drained, and less dense on very dry exposed sites. Requires initial weeding. Cut back hard after flowering when untidy. 'Variegata' has leaves blotched and edged creamy white. Subsp. *hirsuta* is very vigorous, eventually forming dense rampant cover. Height 6–9 in. (15–23 cm). Planting distance 18–24 in. (46–60 cm).
V. *minor*. Smaller leaves but very effective in similar conditions. Forms with variegated foliage and single or double flowers in white, blue or purple. All are useful and attractive. Height 4–6 in. (10–15 cm). Planting distance 15–18 in. (38–46 cm). (See p.6.)

Waldsteinia

W. *ternata*. Perennial carpeter making mats of dark green lobed leaves, with yellow flowers in spring. Excellent cover in any situation and soil. Height 3–4 in. (8–10 cm). Planting distance 12 in. (30 cm).

GROUP B

Evergreens, unless otherwise stated, of medium to slow growth and high to medium density cover. They may be hummock-

26

forming, with a central low stem and many widespreading branches; or carpeting, with rooting prostrate stems; or colonising by spreading underground. They take two seasons to cover the ground, but in time achieve a dense network of branches.

Alyssum

A. saxatilis (Aurinia saxatilis), gold dust. Perennial hummock-former with grey-green leaves and masses of bright yellow flowers in spring. 'Citrinum' has paler flowers. Sun and well-drained soil. Height 9 in. (23 cm). Planting distance 15 in. (38 cm).

Anthemis (see also p.47)

A. cupaniana. Hummock-forming perennial with feathery silver foliage and white daisy flowers in late spring. Sun and well-drained soil. Dislikes wet. Height 9 in. (23 cm). Planting distance 18–24 in. (46–60 cm).

Arabis

A. albida (A. caucasica). Perennial hummock-former with greyish green leaves and white flowers in spring. Does not succeed in poorly drained soil and becomes straggly in shade. 'Flore Pleno' has double flowers. 'Variegata' has cream-edged foliage. Height 5 in. (13 cm). Planting distance 9—15 in. (23–28 cm).

Arctostaphylos

A. uva-ursi, bearberry. Carpeting shrub with dark green leaves and tiny white or pink flowers in April, followed by small red berries. Acid soil in light or dappled shade. Height 6 in. (15 cm). Planting distance 15 in. (38 cm). (See p.28.)

Asarum

A. europaeum. Perennial carpeter with glossy dark green rounded leaves. Useful in shade but not for very dry positions. A. canadense and A. shuttleworthii are less dense. Height 3–4 in. (8–10 cm). Planting distance 9–12 in. (23–30 cm).

Aubrieta

A. deltoidea. Hummock-forming perennial with small grey-green leaves and flowers ranging from purple to pink, in spring. Sun

The bearberry, *Arctostaphylos uva-ursi*, gives year-round interest with flowers, berries and foliage

and well-drained soil. Cut back after flowering when it becomes straggly. Height 3–4 in. (7–10 cm). Planting distance 12 in. (30 cm).

Ballota

B. pseudodictamnus. Hummock-forming woody-based perennial with woolly grey-white rounded leaves. Sun and dry position. Cut back old growth to main rosette in spring. Height 9 in. (23 cm). Planting distance 15 in. (38 cm).

Calluna (heather)

C. vulgaris. Hummock-forming shrub with numerous forms, varying in colour of foliage (some valuable in winter) and of flowers, from white to purple, produced in summer, autumn or early winter. Acid soil. Happier in sun, though tolerant of slight shade. Clip over in spring to maintain compact habit. Height 6–18 in. (15–46 cm). Planting distance 9–18 cm. (23–46 cm). (See p.13.)

Ceanothus

C. thyrsiflorus var. *repens.* Hummock-forming shrub with glossy green leaves and pale blue flowers in early summer. Full sun. Good for banks. Height and planting distance 36 in. (90 cm). (See p.12.)

Left: the ever-popular aubrieta, in this case *A. deltoidea* 'Red Carpet', succeeds in any dry sunny situation
Right: *Convolvulus cneorum* needs a sheltered position but is easily increased from cuttings, which should be taken in summer and placed in gentle heat

Cerastium

C. tomentosum, snow in summer. Carpeting and colonising perennial with silvery grey leaves and white flowers in summer. Full sun. Invasive when established but useful in dry situations. Height 6 in. (15 cm). Planting distance 15 in. (38 cm).

Cistus (rock rose)

C. parviflorus. Hummock-forming shrub with grey-green felted foliage and clear pink flowers in summer. Full sun. *C. salviifolius* 'Prostratus' and *C. lusitanicus* are also good ground covers but less hardy. Height 18–24 in. (46–60 cm). Planting distance 24–30 in. (60–75 cm).

Convolvulus

C. cneorum. Hummock-forming shrub with silvery leaves and white pink-flushed trumpet flowers in summer. Full sun and well-drained soil. Not successful in cold districts. Height 18–24 in. (46–60 cm). Planting distance 24 in. (60 cm).

Cotoneaster (see also p.50)

Shrubs suitable for any soil and position except dense shade.
C. congestus. Carpeter with dull green leaves, small pinkish white flowers in spring and bright red berries. Very dense and compact, though of relatively slow growth. Height 3–4 in. (8–10 cm). Planting distance 12 in. (30 cm).
C. conspicuus. Hummock-forming, with shining dark green leaves, numerous white flowers in early summer and long-lasting scarlet berries. 'Decorus' is more horizontal and spreading, making large dense mounds. Excellent for banks. Height 72 in. (180 cm). Planting distance 60–72 in. (150–180 cm).
C. salicifolius. 'Gnom' is the best of several named forms, a prostrate carpeter with neat foliage and small red fruits in autumn. Grows rapidly to give dense cover. Height 3–4 in. (8–10 cm). Planting distance 18–24 in. (46–60 cm).

Cytisus (broom)

Hummock-forming deciduous shrubs needing full sun and well-drained soil. Slender green twigs give evergreen effect.
C. × kewensis. Downy leaves and creamy white or pale yellow pea flowers in May. Height 12 in. (30 cm). Planting distance 24 in. (60 cm).
C. scoparius var. *prostratus.* Silky-hairy leaves and young twigs and rich yellow flowers in May. Variety of common broom. Growth medium to rapid but weeding necessary in first year. Height 12–15 in. (30–38 cm). Planting distance 36 in. (90 cm).

Daboecia

D. cantabrica, Irish heath. Hummock-forming shrub with sprays of bell-shaped flowers, purple to white depending on form, in summer and autumn. 'Atropurpurea' is vigorous with deep rose-purple flowers. *D. azorica* has rich crimson flowers but is less hardy. Acid soil and sun. Height and planting distance 15–18 in. (38–46 cm).

Dianthus

Garden pinks. Hummock-forming perennials with flowers varying from white to pink to crimson, often scented, in summer. 'Mrs Sinkins', 'Dad's Favourite' and many other forms are suitable. Full sun, alkaline soil. Height 9 in. (23 cm). Planting distance 9–12 in. (23–30 cm).

Euonymus fortunei 'Emerald Gaiety' may develop a more upright habit than other cultivars

Dryas

D. octopetala, mountain avens. Carpeting shrub with small oak-like leaves and white dog-rose flowers in early summer, followed by fluffy seedheeds. Slow-growing at first then forming a dense mat. Full sun. Height 2–3 in. (5–8 cm). Planting distance 12–15 in. (30–38 cm).

Erica (heath)

E. herbacea (*E. carnea*). Hummock-forming or carpeting shrub, with numerous forms in a range of foliage colours and bearing pink or white flowers, mainly in winter. 'Springwood White' and 'Springwood Pink' are spreading and particularly effective. Best in an open position on acid or slightly alkaline soil rich in leaf-mould. May be clipped in spring for denser growth. Other species and hybrids like *E. vagans* and *E.* × *darleyensis* are also good. Height 9 in. (23 cm). Planting distance 15 in. (38 cm).

Euonymus

E. fortunei var. *radicans*. Carpeting or climbing shrub with oval shining green leaves. Makes dense cover in sun or shade. 'Kewensis' is a miniature version with smaller leaves. Other forms, such as 'Emerald and Gold' and 'Emerald Gaiety', with variegated foliage, and 'Coloratus', with leaves turning purple in autumn, can also be used. Height 9 in. (23 cm). Planting distance 12–18 in. (30–46 cm).

E. fortunei f. *carrieri*. Hummock-forming shrub, low and spreading, with small pale green flowers in summer, followed by fruits. Height 24 in. (60 cm). Planting distance 30 in. (75 cm).

× *Gaulnettya*

× *G.* 'Wisley Pearl'. Evergreen colonising shrub with bushy habit and neat foliage, white flowers in early summer and purplish red berries. Hybrid of *Gaultheria* and *Pernettya*. Acid soil with leaf-mould, tolerant of shade. Height 24–36 in. (60–90 cm). Planting distance 24 in. (60 cm).

Genista (broom)

Deciduous shrubs related to *Cytisus* (p.30), requiring a sunny position and well-drained soil. Yellow flowers in May and June.
G. hispanica, Spanish gorse. Hummock-forming, with the crowded twigs and spines giving an evergreen appearance. Height and planting distance 24 in. (60 cm).
G. lydia. More pendulous hummock-forming growth, with grey-green twigs. Height 12–15 in. (30–38 cm). Planting distance 18–21 in. (46–54 cm).
G. pilosa. Carpeter forming a low tangled mass. 'Procumbens' is a prostrate form. Useful on banks and will succeed in light shade. Height 12 in. (30 cm). Planting distance 15–18 in. (38–46 cm).
G. sagittalis. Hummock-forming, sometimes carpeting, with an evergreen effect from the green winged stems. Gives dense cover once established. *G. delphinensis* is like a miniature version. Height 9–12 in. (23–30 cm). Planting distance 12–15 in. (30–38 cm).

× *Halimiocistus*

× *H. sahucii*. Hummock-forming shrub with a profusion of white flowers throughout summer. Natural hybrid of *Cistus* and *Halimium*. Full sun and good drainage. Hardy in all but coldest areas. Height 12 in. (30 cm). Planting distance 21–24 in. (54–60 cm).

Halimium

H. lasianthum. Hummock-forming shrub with greyish leaves and rich yellow flowers with or without a dark central blotch in May. Full sun and well-drained soil. May be damaged in severe winters. Height 12 in. (30 cm). Planting distance 18–24 in. (46–60 cm).

Above: the graceful *Genista lydia* is sometimes hit by late frosts
Below: × *Halimiocistus sahucii*, a dwarf shrub of spreading but close growth

Hebe (see also p.52)

Shrubs for sunny well-drained situations.
H. albicans. Hummock-forming, with grey foliage and spikes of white flowers in summer. 'Pewter Dome' is a fine form with narrower leaves. Height 12 in. (30 cm). Planting distance 18–24 in. (46–60 cm).
H. pinguifolia 'Pagei'. Hummock-forming, occasionally carpeting, with blue-grey foliage and clustered white flowers in May, sometimes repeated in late summer. May die out in centre and requires trimming in April to encourage re-growth. Height 6–9 in. (15–23 cm). Planting distance 15 in. (38 cm).
H. rakaiensis. Hummock-forming, making compact mounds of light green foliage, with white flowers in June and July. *H. vernicosa* is similar, with darker 'varnished' leaves. Height 18–24 in. (46–60 cm). Planting distance 21–24 in. (54–60 cm). (See p.19.)

Helianthemum (sun rose)

Hummock-forming shrubs needing full sun and good drainage. Cut back after flowering
H. nummularium 'Amy Baring'. Green leaves and deep yellow flowers in summer. Forms dense spreading mats. Height 4–6 in. (10–15 cm). Planting distance 12–18 in. (30–46 cm). (see p.19.)
Garden hybrids. Green or grey foliage and single or double flowers in many colours. 'Wisley Pink' and 'Wisley Primrose' are dense grey-leaved forms. Ideal for a sunny bank. Height 6–9 in. (15–23 cm). Planting distance 12–18 in. (30–46 cm).

Hypericum (see also p.25)

H. cerastoides. Carpeting shrub with greyish hairy leaves and bright yellow flowers in May. Full sun and well-drained soil. Height 3 in. (8 cm). Planting distance 9–12 in. (23–30 cm).
H. × moserianum. Hummock-forming, slightly colonising shrub with large golden yellow flowers from July to October. Stands some shade but prefers sun. Often killed back in winter. Height 18 in. (46 cm). Planting distance 18–21 in. (46–54 cm).

Iberis (candytuft)

I. sempervirens. Hummock-forming shrub with narrow dark green leaves and plentiful white flowers from April to June. 'Snowflake' is a compact form. Sunny well-drained spot. Height 9–12 in. (23–30 cm). Planting distance 12–15 in. (30–38 cm). (See p.62.)

Above: the delightful *Hebe pinguifolia* 'Pagei' forms a low mat of blue-grey foliage
Below: the pale pink orange-centred flowers of *Helianthemum* 'Wisley pink' are borne from late May to the end of June

The prostrate *Juniperus communis* 'Depressa Aurea' becomes golden yellow in summer, particularly when planted in full sun, and bronze in autumn

Juniperus (juniper)

Hummock-forming shrubs, sometimes carpeting or rooting down. Particularly useful on poor soils, including chalk, and in hot dry situations.

J. communis var. *jackii*. Sea-green foliage and low spreading branches. Open sunny position. Subsp. *depressa* and other forms like 'Depressa Aurea', 'Dumosa', 'Effusa' and 'Repanda', with variously coloured foliage, are equally useful. Height 6–9 in. (15–23 cm). Planting distance 24 in. (60 cm).

J. conferta. Bright green prickly leaves and prostrate habit. Tolerates some shade. Height 6–9 in. (15–23 cm). Planting distance 24 in. (60 cm).

J. horizontalis. Available in several forms with blue-grey, bronze or green foliage. Makes thick creeping mats eventually but requires weeding in early years. Sun. Height 6 in. (15 cm). Planting distance 18–24 in. (46–60 cm).

J. × *media* 'Pfitzeriana'. Green and grey-green leaves on wide-spreading arching branches. Will withstand dense shade of trees. Forms with golden foliage are less vigorous. Height 36 in. (90 cm). Planting distance 48–72 in. (1.2–1.8 m).

J. sabina var. *tamariscifolia*. Bright green leaves on closely tiered branches. Dense cover, though relatively slow. Accepts partial shade. Height 15–18 in. (38–46 cm). Planting distance 24–30 in. (60–75 cm).

Leucothoe

L. fontanesiana. Carpeting shrub with leathery green leaves turning bronze in autumn and clusters of white flowers along arching branches in May. Acid leafy soil and shade. Height 36 in. (90 cm). Planting distance 30–36 in. (75–90 cm).

Lithospermum

L. diffusum (Lithodora diffusa). Hummock-forming, trailing shrub with vivid blue flowers in early summer. 'Heavenly Blue' and 'Grace Ward' have larger flowers. Acid soil. Will grow in some shade but best in a sunny open position. Tends to die out in patches. Height 9 in. (23 cm). Planting distance 12–15 in. (30–38 cm).

Lonicera (honeysuckle) (see also p.59)

L. pileata. Hummock-forming, sometimes carpeting shrub with neat glossy dark green foliage, occasionally producing clusters of translucent violet berries. Any well-drained soil in sun or shade. The related *L. nitida* 'Graziosa' is similar. Height 18 in. (46 cm). Planting distance 24–30 in. (60–75 cm).

Lithospermum diffusum 'Heavenly Blue' should be lightly trimmed after flowering

Mahonia

M. aquifolium. Colonising shrub with polished dark green pinnate leaves, golden yellow flowers in early spring and blue-black berries. Succeeds in shade and dry soil if mulched annually. Cut back in April each year to encourage dense habit. *M. repens* var. *rotundifolia* is taller and gives equally dense cover when mature, though both may be slow to establish. Height and planting distance 24 in. (60 cm).

Osteospermum

O. jucundum (Dimorphotheca barberiae). Hummock-forming shrubby perennial with slender light green leaves and mauve-pink daisy flowers throughout summer. 'Compactum' is mat-forming and particularly suitable. 'Nairobi Purple' has deep purple flowers but is less hardy. Excellent summer cover in sunny well-drained site. Not for cold wet districts. Height 6–9 in. (15–23 cm). Planting distance 15–18 in. (38–46 cm).

Pachysandra

P. terminalis. Carpeting shrub with diamond-shaped leaves at ends of the stems and spikes of greenish flowers in spring. Very useful in shade. 'Variegata', with white-striped leaves, is slightly less vigorous. Height 3–4 in. (8–10 cm). Planting distance 9–12 in. (23–30 cm).

Parahebe

P. catarractae. Hummock-forming deciduous shrub with white or blue-purple flowers in late summer. Open sunny position in well-drained soil. *P. lyallii* is similar, with smaller foliage and more prostrate, often carpeting. Height 9 in. (23 cm). Planting distance 12 in. (30 cm).

Pernettya

Colonising shrubs forming dense thickets. Acid soil and full sun. *P. mucronata.* Wiry thickly leafy stems and numerous white heather-like flowers in May and June, followed by variously coloured berries lasting through winter. Several forms available. Should be planted in groups, including a male form, to ensure berries. Height 24–36 in. (60–90 cm). Planting distance 24 in. (60 cm).

Left: *Pachysandra terminalis* 'Variegata' flourishes in any moist soil
Right: the variable *Parahebe catarractae* makes effective ground cover
in sun

P. prostrata subsp. *pentlandii*. Dense dark glossy green leaves,
white flowers in early summer and black berries. Spreading
growth and tolerant of slight shade. Height 12–18 in. (30–46 cm).
Planting distance 15 in. (38 cm).

Phlomis

P. fruticosa, Jerusalem sage. Hummock-forming shrub with
woolly grey-green foliage and whorls of bright yellow flowers in
summer. Gives dense cover in a sunny sheltered position and best
in warm areas. *P. chrysophylla* differs in its lower habit and
golden green foliage. Both ideal for a dry sunny bank. Height
36 in. (90 cm). Planting distance 30–36 in. (75–90 cm).

Potentilla (see also p.54)

P. fruticosa, shrubby cinquefoil. Hummock-forming deciduous
shrub with small divided leaves and yellow flowers from early
summer to autumn. Represented in gardens by numerous
hybrids, many of spreading dense habit, such as 'Longacre', 'Eliz-
abeth' and 'Gold Drop'. *P. davurica* var. *mandshurica* has grey-
green leaves and white flowers. Open sunny position in any
reasonably drained soil. Height 15–18 in. (38–46 cm). Planting distance 24–30 in. (60–75 cm).

Left: the gold- and purple-leaved forms of common sage, *Salvia officinalis*, go well together
Right: the well-known *Senecio* 'Sunshine' is a good shrubby ground cover for seaside gardens

Prunus

P. laurocerasus 'Otto Luyken'. Hummock-forming shrub with narrow glossy green leaves and small white flowers in April. A low compact form of cherry laurel. The spreading 'Zabeliana' and 'Schipkaensis' are equally good ground cover, tolerant of dense shade, even from trees, and almost any soil. Height 36 in. (90 cm). Planting distance 36–48 in. (90–120 cm).

Salvia

S. officinalis, common sage. Hummock-forming shrub with soft grey green aromatic leaves and purple flowers in summer. Full sun and well-drained soil. May suffer in harsh winters. Can be trimmed in late spring to keep compact. 'Purpurascens' and 'Icterina', purple and golden sage, are slightly less vigorous. Height 12–18 in. (30–46 cm). Planting distance 18–24 in. (46–60 cm).

Senecio

S. 'Sunshine'. Hummock-forming shrub with grey foliage and yellow daisy flowers in summer. Sun and good drainage. Height 36 in. (90 cm). Planting distance 36–48 in. (90–120 cm).

GROUP C

Deciduous, unless otherwise stated, herbaceous perennials of medium to slow growth and high to medium density cover, forming clumps as the roots gradually increase. Relatively slow but steady ground covers, providing a thick canopy of leaves, especially in summer.

Acanthus

A. mollis var. *latifolius*, bear's breeches. Bold rich green leaves and tall mauve flower spikes in summer. Prefers sun but will tolerate shade. Spreads from suckers and can be invasive. Height and planting distance 36 in. (90 cm).

Alchemilla

A. mollis, lady's mantle. Fresh green wavy-edged leaves and frothy yellow-green flowers in summer. Succeeds in sun or shade and any soil. Cut off flowers to prevent seeding and divide if necessary after about five years. Height 6–9 in. (15–23 cm). Planting distance 15–18 in. (38–46 cm). (See p.43.)

Bergenia

Species and hybrids. Large evergreen foliage, often changing colour in winter, and heads of purple to pink flowers in spring. Any situation and soil, though more straggling in deep shade. Increasing from creeping rhizomes. Avoid *B. ciliata* and *B.* 'Ballawley', which can be damaged by frost and wind. Height 5–12 in. (13–30 cm). Planting distance 9–24 in. (23–60 cm).

Brunnera

B. macrophylla. Big cabbagey leaves and blue forget-me-not flowers in spring. Best in shade as foliage is liable to scorch in sun. Height 12 in. (30 cm). Planting distance 15–18 in. (38–46 cm).

Geranium (cranesbill) (see also p.51)

Versatile and dense ground covers with attractive foliage and flowers, mostly produced in summer. Thriving in any reasonable soil and positions ranging from full sun to deep shade.
G. endressi. Divided light green leaves and continuous pink flowers. 'Wargrave Pink' has brighter pink flowers. The hybrid 'Claridge

Druce' is even more vigorous, with magenta-pink flowers. Both spread from the central rosette and retain old foliage in winter. Height 12–21 in. (30–54 cm). Planting distance 12–15 in. (30–38 cm). *G. himalayense*. Dark green leaves and violet-blue flowers. Spreads from suckers. The hybrid 'Johnson's Blue' has paler blue flowers. Height 9–12 in. (23–30 cm). Planting distance 12–15 in. (30–38 cm). *G.* × *magnificum*. Hairy leaves, often tinted in autumn, and violet-blue flowers. Withstands hot sun. *G. ibericum* and *G. platypetalum* are similar. Height 9–12 in. (23–30 cm). Planting distance 12–15 in. (30–38 cm).

G. phaeum, mourning widow. Maroon to white flowers in late spring. Excellent in deep shade, as are *G. punctatum*, with mauve-purple flowers, and *G. nodosum*, with a succession of small lilac flowers above glossy green leaves. Height 12 in. (30 cm). Planting distance 15–18 in. (38–46 cm).

G. psilostemon. Deeply cut leaves and bright magenta flowers with dark centres. Best in open position. Height 30 in. (75 cm). Planting distance 24–36 in. (60–90 cm). (see cover.)

G. sanguineum. Dark green leaves and plentiful flowers of deep magenta to white. Prefers some sun. Subsp. *lancastriense* is more prostrate with pink veined flowers. Spreading by suckers. Height 6–9 in. (15–23 cm). Planting distance 12–15 in. (30–38 cm).

G. sylvaticum. White, pink or lavender-blue flowers in May. Seeds freely. Very tolerant of shade. Height 12–15 in. (30–38 cm). Planting distance 15–18 in. (38–46 cm).

Geum

G. 'Borisii'. Rich green hairy leaves in a dense mound and bright orange flowers in early summer. Sun and any soil. Height 6–9 in. (15–23 cm). Planting distance 12 in. (30 cm). (See p.44.)

Hemerocallis (daylily)

Species and garden hybrids. Arching grassy foliage giving dense summer cover and lily flowers in a range of colours, especially yellows, in summer. Sun or partial shade in any soil. Most form compact clumps, but *H. flava* and *H. fulva* have running roots which can be invasive. Height 18–24 in. (46–60 cm). Planting distance 18 in. (46 cm). (See p.23.)

Hosta

Indispensable foliage plants for dense shade, doing equally well

Above: the charming lady's mantle, *Alchemilla mollis*, will proliferate in almost any situation
Below: *Geranium × magnificum*, often known by the name of one of its parents, *G. ibericum*

Geum 'Borisii' forms dense clumps which should be divided every few years to keep it healthy

in sun and not fussy about soil. Thick summer cover. Lily-shaped flowers, generally lilac-coloured, in summer.

H. crispula. Long pointed spreading leaves margined white. Height 12 in. (30 cm). Planting distance 15–18 in. (38–46 cm).

H. decorata. Blunt broad leaves edged in white. Like most hostas, should be divided after five years rather than ten. Height 9–12 in. (23–30 cm). Planting distances 15 in. (38 cm).

H. fortunei. 'Albopicta' and 'Obscura Marginata' have yellow-margined leaves. 'Hyacintha' has blue-green leaves. 'Obscura' has handsome green leaves. *H. fortunei f. rugosa* has corrugated leaves. Height and planting distance 18 in. (46 cm).

H. plantaginea. Pale green glossy arching foliage and scented white trumpet flowers in late summer. Flowers best in warm moist situation. Height and planting distance 15 in. (38 cm).

H. rectifolia 'Tall Boy'. Long pointed leaves and notable lilac flowers. Vigorous growth. Height and planting distance 18 in. (46 cm). (See p.62.)

H. sieboldiana. Huge grey-green leaves, blue-grey and crinkled in var. *elegans*, yellow-margined in 'Frances Williams'. Height 18 in. (46 cm). Planting distance 18–24 in. (46–60 cm).

H. undulata var. *erromena*. Long glossy green leaves and tall spikes of purple flowers. Var. *undulata* and var. *univittata* have smaller variegated foliage and are less dense. Height and planting distance 18 in. (46 cm). (See p.14.)

H. ventricosa. Dark shining green leaves and rich violet-purple flowers. 'Variegata' and 'Aureomaculata' are good variegated forms but slightly less vigorous. Height 15 in. (38 cm). Planting distance 18 in. (46 cm).

Iris

I. foetidissima. Dark green arching evergreen foliage, with insignificant flowers followed by orange seed pods in autumn. Thrives in any position unless badly drained, including deep shade and dry soil. Spreads from rhizomes. 'Citrina' has larger pale yellow flowers in early summer and good pods of red berries. Height 18 in. (46 cm). Planting distance 12–15 in. (30–38 cm).

Liriope

L. muscari. Grass-like evergreen leaves and spikes of lavender flowers in autumn. Sunny dry situation. Height 9 in. (23 cm). Planting distance 9–12 in. (23–30 cm). (See p.46.)

Nepeta

N. × *faassenii*, catmint. Small greyish leaves and sprays of lavender flowers throughout summer. Prefers full sun and good drainage and less hardy in cold damp districts. Cut back old growths in spring. Height 9 in. (23 cm). Planting distance 12 in. (30 cm).

Origanum

O. vulgare 'Aureum'. Bright golden yellow foliage developing in spring to give good summer cover. Needs open well-drained site. *O. vulgare*, wild marjoram, has dark green leaves and tiny mauve flowers in summer. Height 6 in. (15 cm). Planting distance 12 in. (30 cm).

Pachyphragma

P. macrophyllum. Rounded glossy bright green leaves and white flowers in May. Likes shade in fairly moist soil. Height 6–9 in. (15–23 cm). Planting distance 12–15 in. (30–38 cm).

Left: *Liriope muscari* has arching shiny leaves and flowers most freely in sun
Right: the red bells of *Pulmonaria rubra* appear at the end of January and continue until March

Polygonum (knotweed) (see also p.54)

P. campanulatum. Winter rosettes form widespreading trails of soft green foliage, with long-lasting pink flowers in summer. Spreads rapidly from creeping roots but not invasive. Prefers moist soil and is content with some shade. Height and planting distance 18–24 in. (46–60 cm).

Pulmonaria (lungwort)

Species and hybrids. Almost all are effective easy ground covers for sun or shade, preferably in moist soil. Spreading by roots and also from seed. They flower in early spring. Height 5–6 in. (13–15 cm). Planting distance 12 in. (30 cm).
P. angustifolia. Bristly leaves and blue flowers. 'Mawson's Variety' and 'Azurea' are good forms. (See p.22.)
P. officinalis, spotted dog. Evergreen leaves spotted and blotched with white and pink flowers turning blue. *P. saccharata* is similar.
P. rubra. Evergreen leaves and early red flowers.

GROUP D

Deciduous or evergreen plants of rapid to medium growth and high to medium density cover, either carpeters which root on the surface, or colonisers which spread underground. Most cover the ground quickly, but make thinner growth initially than other groups and need two seasons to achieve a dense canopy.

46

Acaena

A. novae-zelandiae. Deciduous carpeting perennial with rounded hairy leaves and inconspicuous purplish flower heads in summer. Roots at the nodes. Sun and well-drained soil. Other species like *A. caesiiglauca* are also effective but variable in density of cover. Height 3–4 in. (8–10 cm). Planting distance 15–28 in. (38–70 cm).

Ajuga

A. reptans, bugle. Evergreen perennial carpeter with dark green leaves and spikes of blue flowers in spring. 'Atropurpurea', with glossy reddish purple foliage, and 'Multicolor', with purple, pink, cream and bronze foliage, colour best in sun. 'Jungle Beauty' is a large green-leaved vigorous form. Sun or partial shade and moist soil. Needs good conditions to avoid becoming bare in the centre and requires feeding. Height 2–5 in. (5–13 cm). Planting distance 9–15 in. (23–38 cm).

Antennaria

A. dioica. Evergreen carpeting perennial with greyish leaves and small white flowers in summer. Sun and well drained soil. Will form a close mat but is somewhat slow-growing and needs weeding in first year. Height 1–2 in. (2–5 cm). Planting distance 9 in. (23 cm).

Anthemis (see also p.27)

A. nobilis (*Chamaemelum nobile*), chamomile. Evergreen perennial carpeter with feathery leaves and white daisy flowers in summer, both aromatic. Sun and light or sandy soil. Apt to die out in patches but gaps can be filled with young plants. A useful alternative to grass and may be mown in the same way. 'Treneague', which is non-flowering and has dense mossy foliage, is best for a lawn. Height 1–3 in. (2–8 cm). Planting distance 9–15 in. (23–38 cm). (See p.48.)

Artemisia

A. canescens (of gardens). Evergreen colonising perennial with silver-grey filigree foliage. Full sun or growth will be sparse. *A. stelleriana,* dusty miller, has broad divided grey-white downy leaves. Height 9–12 in. (23–30 cm). Planting distance 15–18 in. (38–46 cm). (See p.48.)

Above: *Anthemis nobilis* 'Treneague' (left) makes a lovely scented lawn or clothing for a bank; the striking *Artemisia canescens* (right) is happy in any ordinary soil
Below: the native hard fern, *Blechnum spicant* (left), prefers lime-free soil; *Centaurea* 'John Coutts' (right) appreciates a well-drained position

Arundinaria (bamboo)

A. viridistriata. Evergreen coloniser with leaves of dark green striped with rich yellow. Spreads from creeping rhizome and may be less dense at edges of clump. Succeeds in sun or moderate shade. Height and planting distance 24 in. (60 cm).

Asperula

A. odorata (*Galium odoratum*), sweet woodruff. Deciduous colonising perennial quickly making dense drifts of rich green foliage, with scented white flowers in May. Thrives in shade and can be invasive. Height 4–5 in. (10–13 cm). Planting distance 24 in. (60 cm).

Blechnum

B. spicant, hard fern. Evergreen colonising fern with dark green ladder-like fronds. Prefers moist leafy soil, lime-free. Relatively slow growth but useful in shade of trees and shrubs. Height 9–15 in. (23–38 cm). Planting distance 12 in. (30 cm).

Campanula (bellflower)

Colonising perennials with blue flowers in summer. Will accept some shade but better in sun, in well-drained soil.
C. portenschlagiana. Deciduous, with clusters of blue-purple bell-shaped flowers. Height 3–4 in. (8–10 cm). Planting distance 9–12 in. (23–30 cm).
C. poscharskyana. Dense evergreen leaves and trailing stems with starry lilac-blue flowers. Can be invasive. 'E.K. Toogood' is less rampant. Height 3–4 in. (8–10 cm).

Centaurea

C. 'John Coutts'. Deciduous perennial coloniser with grey foliage and pink knapweed flowers in early summer. Full sun. Height 6 in. (15 cm). Planting distance 12–15 in. (30–38 cm).

Ceratostigma

C. plumbaginoides. Deciduous colonising perennial with leaves becoming red-tinted in autumn at the same time as the dark blue flower heads appear. Sun in well-drained soil. Height 9 in. (23 cm). Planting distance 12–15 in. (30–38 cm). (See p.51.)

Cornus

C. canadensis, creeping dogwood. Deciduous perennial coloniser with leaves often changing colour in autumn and white four-bracted flowers in summer. Spreads by underground shoots. Acid moist soil and partial shade. Height 4–6 in. (10–15 cm). Planting distance 12–15 in. (30–38 cm).

Cotoneaster (see also p.30)

C. dammeri. Evergreen carpeting shrub with slender creeping stems and coral-red berries in autumn. Spreading thin growth at first, later dense, but needs weeding for first two years. Almost any soil and situation. 'Coral Beauty' is less ground-hugging. Height 3–4 in. (8–10 cm). Planting distance 24 in. (60 cm). (see p.14.)

Cotula

C. squalida. Evergreen carpeting perennial with ferny bronze-green leaves and creamy yellow button flowers in summer. Makes a mat of foliage in dry or damp soil, sun or shade, and is fairly invasive. Height 1 in. (2 cm). Planting distance 9 in. (23 cm).

Dicentra

D. formosa. Deciduous perennial coloniser with light green ferny leaves and mauve-pink locket flowers in late spring. Shade and moist soil. Height 9 in. (23 cm). Planting distance 15 in. (38 cm).

Duchesnea

D. indica (Fragaria indica). Deciduous carpeting perennial with dark green strawberry-like foliage, yellow flowers in spring and red fruits. Only for rougher positions where it cannot smother smaller plants. Height 3 in. (8 cm). Planting distance 15 in. (38 cm).

Epimedium

Colonising perennials with lobed leaves, often attractively tinted in spring and autumn, and variously coloured flowers in spring. Excellent in sun or shade and any soil, but relatively slow.
E. perralderianum. Evergreen, with large shining green leaves and bright yellow flowers. *E. pinnatum* var. *colchicum* and *E.* × *perralchicum* are similar. Height and planting distance 12 in. (30 cm). (See p.2.)

50

Left: *Ceratostigma plumbaginoides* flowers continuously in September and October
Right: the foliage of *Epimedium* × *rubrum* is handsomely tinted when young, later turning pale green

E. × *versicolor.* Deciduous, with coppery leaves in spring and pink flowers. 'Sulphureum' has yellow flowers and is more vigorous. *E.* × *rubrum*, with crimson flowers, is equally good. Cut off old leaf stalks in spring. Height and planting distance 9 in. (23 cm).

Euphorbia (spurge)

E. robbiae. Evergreen perennial coloniser with rosettes of dark green leaves and tall spires of greenish flowers in spring. Sometimes slow to establish but then spreads freely by underground runners. Sun or shade in any soil. Height 15 in. (38 cm). Planting distance 18 in. (46 cm).

Gaultheria

G. procumbens, creeping wintergreen. Evergreen colonising shrub with leathery glossy leaves, aromatic and turning reddish in autumn, tiny pinkish white flowers in July and August and vivid red berries. Acid soil in shade. Happy in dry conditions once established. Height 6 in. (15 cm). Planting distance 12–15 in. (30–38 cm).

Geranium (cranesbill) (see also p.41)

Deciduous carpeting perennials with rounded divided leaves and saucer-shaped flowers. Tolerant of many situations and soils.

51

Left: *Geranium* 'Russell Prichard' is valuable for its very long
flowering season

G. macrorrhizum. Light green aromatic leaves, changing colour in
autumn, and magenta, pink or white flowers according to the
form in late spring. Extremely dense cover. Height 9–12 in.
(23–30 cm). Planting distance 12–15 in. (30–38 cm).
G. 'Russell Prichard'. Greyish green leaves and continuous pink
flowers from July onwards. Sends out dense trails of foliage in
summer, dying back to the rootstock in winter. Requires full sun
and good drainage, and may be slightly tender in cold areas. *G.*
wallichianum has a similar habit, is hardy and does not mind
shade. 'Buxton's Variety' has blue flowers with white eyes. Height
6–9 in. (15–23 cm). Planting distance 12–15 in. (30–38 cm).

Glechoma

G. hederacea (*Nepeta hederacea*) 'Variegata'. Evergreen carpeting
perennial with rounded green white-splashed leaves and lavender-blue flowers in spring. Variegated form of ground ivy – a
rampageous weed – and less vigorous, needing some weeding in
first year or two. Useful in shade. Height 3–4 in. (8–10 cm).
Planting distance 18–24 in. (46–60 cm).

Hebe (see also p.34)

H. chathamica. Evergreen carpeting shrub with green foliage and
white or violet-tinged flowers in June. Prostrate branches
spreading rapidly and rooting. Sun and well-drained soil. Height

4–6 in. (10–15 cm). Planting distance 18–24 in. (46–60 cm).

Lamium

L. maculatum. Evergreen perennial carpeter with dark green white-striped leaves and magenta, pink or white flowers in early summer. Will thrive in deep shade. Height 3–4 in. (8—10 cm). Planting distance 12–15 in. (30–38 cm).

Luzula

L. maxima (L. sylvatica), woodrush. Evergreen colonising grass, spreading quickly to form solid mats. Rampant but ideal for dense dry shade, steep banks and other difficult places. 'Variegata' has cream-edged leaves and is slightly less invasive. Height 12 in. (30 cm). Planting distance 12–15 in. (30–38 cm).

Lysimachia

L. nummularia, creeping Jenny. Evergreen carpeting perennial with bright green rounded leaves and yellow flowers in summer. Moist sites in sun or shade. Needs weeding in first year. 'Aurea' has golden leaves but may be scorched in sun. Height 1–2 in. (2–5 cm). Planting distance 12–15 in. (30–38 cm). (See p.61.)

Maiaenthemum

M. bifolium. Deciduous perennial coloniser with smooth green leaves and creamy white flowers in late spring. Cool soil with leaf-mould, in shade. Height 4–5 in. (10–13 cm). Planting distance 12–15 in. (30–38 cm).

Meuhlenbeckia

M. axillaris. Deciduous colonising shrub with tiny round leaves and minute pale green flowers in July. Threadlike stems develop into a tangled mass and can smother small plants. Best in full sun. Height 6–9 in. (15–23 cm). Planting distance 18 in. (46 cm).

Omphalodes

O. cappodocica. Deciduous colonising perennial with glossy leaves and blue flowers in early summer. Best in shade and rich soil but withstands sun given moist conditions. *O. verna* is smaller. Height 6 in. (15 cm). Planting distance 12 in. (30 cm).

Oxalis

O. oregana. Deciduous colonising perennial with rich green clover leaves and white to purplish pink flowers in spring. Fairly dense summer cover in leafy woodland soil and tolerant of deep shade. Increases from rhizomeś but not as invasive as *O. acetosella*, wood sorrel, or *O. rubra*.

Phlox

P. subulata and *P. douglasii* hybrids. Deciduous perennial carpeters with needle-like foliage and flowers ranging from violet to pink and white in late spring. 'Temiscaming', magenta, 'May Snow', white, 'Chattahoochee', lavender-blue, and many others can be recommended. Full sun and good drainage. Height 3–4 in. (8–10 cm). Planting distance 9–12 in. (23–30 cm).

Polygonum (knotweed) (see also p.46)

Deciduous carpeting perennials with narrow bright green leaves and erect spikes of pink flowers.
P. affine. 'Darjeeling Red' and 'Superbum' are reliable, bearing richly coloured flowers in summer. 'Donald Lowndes' tends to die out in patches. Sun or light shade, preferably in moist soil. Height 2–3 in. (5–8 cm). Planting distance 9–12 in. (23–30 cm).
P. vacciniifolium. Valuable for late summer flowering. Sometimes slow to establish but then makes dense cover. Open sunny position. Height 3–4 in. (8–10 cm). Planting distance 9–12 in. (23–30 cm).

Potentilla (see also p.39)

Deciduous carpeting perennials for well-drained soils.
P. alba. Leaves green above, grey below, and white orange-centred flowers in spring and autumn. Will accept some shade. Dense when established. Height 2–3 in. (5–8 cm). Planting distance 9–12 in. (23–30 cm).
P. argentea. Similar leaves and sulphur-yellow flowers in spring and autumn. Needs sun. May die back in patches in winter. Height 2–3 in. (5–8 cm). Planting distance 9–12 in. (23–30 cm).

Prunella

P. grandiflora. Evergreen perennial carpeter with hairy dark green leaves and pink or white flowers in July. 'Loveliness' has

Rubus tricolor will send out its long trailing stems in the shadiest places, even under beech trees

rich pink flowers. Sun or partial shade. Not for dry sandy soil. Height 3–4 in. (8–10 cm). Planting distance 12 in. (30 cm).

Rubus

Evergreen carpeting shrubs related to blackberry, with small white flowers in summer, followed by red fruits. Succeeding in sun or deep shade, in all but poorly drained soils.
R. calycinoides. Wrinkled three-lobed dark green leaves. Prostrate and spreading, making firmly matted cover. Height 2—3 in. (5–8 cm). Planting distance 12–15 in. (30–38 cm).
R. tricolor. Heart-shaped leaves and very bristly stems. Grows strongly but needs weeding at first. Height 12 in. (30 cm). Planting distance 36–38 in. (90–120 cm).

Sarcococca

S. humilis. Evergreen colonising shrub with small glossy green foliage, fragrant white flowers in February and black fruits. Neat dense habit, increasing by suckers to form clumps. Likes a shady position in leaf-enriched soil. Height 9–15 in. (23–38 cm). Planting distance 12–15 in. (30–38 cm).

Saxifraga (saxifrage)

Mossy hybrids. Evergreen perennial carpeters with fresh green

Left: the mossy saxifrages, such as 'Four Winds', grow into large rounded cushions
Right: the dainty *Stephanandra incisa* 'Crispa' may be pruned in March to keep it tidy

leaves, sometimes bronze or grey, and flowers from white to deep red in early summer. Usually make thick mats or mounds of foliage. Best in well-drained soil in cool, slightly shady situation. Height 2–3 in. (5–8 cm). Planting distance 12 in. (30 cm).

Sedum (stonecrop)

Evergreen carpeting perennials with smooth fleshy leaves and heads of starry flowers in summer. Sun and reasonable drainage, thriving in poor soil.
S. *spathulifolium*. Purplish or greyish white leaves and tiny yellow flowers. S. *spurium* has green leaves and pink flowers. 'Green Mantle' is non-flowering and an excellent carpeter. Height 2–3 in. (5–8 cm). Planting distance 9–12 in. (23–30 cm)

Stachys

S. *olympica* 'Silver Carpet'. Evergreen perennial carpeter with velvety silver foliage. Non-flowering form of lamb's ears. Sun and well-drained soil. Height 3–4 in. (8–10 cm). Planting distance 12–15 in. (30–38 cm). (See p.8.)

Stephanandra

S. *incisa* 'Crispa'. Deciduous carpeting shrub with deeply incised fresh green leaves, crisped when young and turning orange in autumn. Forms a low network of arching branches. Any but very dry soils in sun or slight shade. Height 18–24 in. (46–60 cm). Planting distance 36 in. (90 cm).

Symphoricarpos

S. × chenaultii 'Hancock'. Deciduous colonising and carpeting shrub with pink fruits in autumn. Makes mounds of arching branches. Almost any situation, though thinner in shade. Height 18–24 in. (46–60 cm). Planting distance 36 in. (90 cm).

Symphytum (comfrey)

S. grandiflorum. Deciduous carpeting and colonising perennial with broad hairy leaves and creamy bell flowers in spring. 'Hidcote Pink' and 'Hidcote Blue' are taller. Excellent and rapid cover under trees and shrubs, preferably in moist soil. Height 6 in. (15 cm). Planting distance 12 in. (30 cm).

Tellima

T. grandiflora. Evergreen perennial carpeter with rounded green leaves becoming bronzed in winter and sprays of creamy flowers in late spring. 'Purpurea' has foliage turning purplish in winter and pinkish flowers. Sun or shade in any except poorly drained soils. Height 6 in. (15 cm). Planting distance 12 in. (30 cm).

Thymus (thyme)

T. serpyllum. Evergreen carpeting shrub with tiny dark green leaves on trailing stems and dense rounded heads of rosy purple flowers in summer. Forms available with white, lilac or pink flowers, including 'Pink Chintz'. Full sun and good drainage. Height 1 in. (2 cm). Planting distance 9 in. (23 cm).

Tiarella

T. cordifolia, foam flower. Evergreen carpeting perennial with rich green leaves, bronze-tinted in winter, and a froth of creamy white flowers in spring. T. wherryi has pinkish white flowers but is slower. Leaf-enriched soil in shade. Height 3–4 in. (8–10 cm). Planting distance 12–15 in. (30–38 cm). (See p.9.)

Vaccinium

V. vitis-idaea, cowberry. Evergreen colonising shrub with boxlike shiny green leaves, burnished in winter, and white or pinkish bell flowers in summer, following by dark red berries. Acid humus-enriched soil and shade. Height 6 in. (15 cm). Planting distance 9–12 in. (23–30 cm).

Vancouveria

V. hexandra. Deciduous colonising perennial with divided foliage and sprays of white flowers in spring, similar to *Epimedium* (p.50). Best in shade and fairly rich soil. Will tolerate open position but less vigorous. Height 6 in. (15 cm). Planting distance 12 in. (30 cm).

Veronica

V. prostrata. Evergreen perennial carpeter forming mats of prostrate stems, with dense clusters of deep blue flowers in May and June. 'Kapitan' and 'Spode Blue' are good forms. Sun and well-drained soil. Height 1–2 in. (2–5 cm). Planting distance 9–12 in. (23–30 cm).

Viola

Useful perennials for any well-drained soil and tolerant of shade. Height 3–4 in. (8–10 cm). Planting distance 9–12 in. (23–30 cm). *V. cornuta.* Evergreen carpeter with thick light green foliage and masses of lilac-purple or white flowers in summer. Succeeds in

Viola 'Huntercombe Purple' can be cut over after blooming to encourage further flowers

cool open situation with good drainage. *V*. 'Huntercombe Purple' has rich purple flowers and enjoys the same conditions. Other equally effective forms are 'Haslemere', lavender-pink, 'Connie', white, and 'Martin', deep purple.

V. labradorica. Evergreen coloniser with purple-flushed foliage and lavender-blue violet flowers in spring. Good in dense shade or sun. Runs freely underground and can become a nuisance. (See p.9.)

V. obliqua (*V. cucullata*). Deciduous coloniser with foliage slowly forming compact mats to give dense summer cover and bearing purple or white flowers in early summer. Good in any but boggy soils and in dense shade.

OTHERS

Clematis

C. orientalis. Deciduous climbing shrub with twining leaf stalks and yellow bell flowers in late summer and autumn. Grows rapidly to give dense tangled mass of growth in sun or moderate shade and any reasonable soil. Good for banks. Height 24 in. (60 cm). Planting distance 6 ft (1.8 m).

Lonicera (see also p.37)

L. japonica var. *halliana.* Evergreen climbing shrub with twining stems and fragrant honeysuckle flowers, white then yellow, from July onwards. Very vigorous, often rooting as it sprawls, and quickly making a dense canopy. Only for large areas where it cannot strangle other plants. Sun or shade. *L. henryi* has purplish red flowers in midsummer and may be used in the same way. Height 12 in. (30 cm). Planting distance 36 in. (90 cm).

Rhododendron

Hummock-forming, sometimes carpeting or colonising, evergreen shrubs, with beautiful flowers from spring to summer and often with attractive foliage. Slow-growing but eventually achieving good cover. Acid woodland conditions in humus-enriched soil. Many species and hybrids are suitable, as are some Japanese azaleas. (For further details, see the Wisley handbook, *Rhododendrons.*)

Rosa (rose)

Only a few roses are really effective and these will give thick cover, although requiring weeding for the first two seasons after

The widespreading, prickly *Rosa* 'Max Graf' is only suitable for larger gardens

Rosa (rose)

Only a few roses are really effective and these will give thick cover, although requiring weeding for the first two seasons after planting. Low-growing shrub roses, such as 'Bonica', 'Ferdy', 'Rosy Cushion' and 'Smarty', are particularly suitable for smaller gardens, growing about 36 in. (90 cm) high and 48 in. (120 cm) across. Full sun.

R. × paulii. Deciduous hummock-former, making a dense mound of very prickly interlacing branches with clusters of starry white scented flowers in midsummer. Far-spreading but useful for banks and large areas. Height 5 ft (1.5 m). Planting distance 15 ft (4.5 m).

R. wichuraiana. Carpeting rambler rose, evergreen or deciduous, with smooth dark green leaves and very fragrant white flowers in August and later. Very low, with almost thornless trails developing up to 10 ft (3 m) in a season and eventually spreading far. 'Max Graf' is a slightly taller evergreen hybrid with bright pink flowers in summer. More modern hybrids are 'Pheasant', 'Partridge', and 'Grouse'. 'Temple Bells' has white flowers and at Wisley has fully covered the ground in two seasons, planted 36–48 in. (90–120 cm) apart. Height 18 in. (46 cm). Planting distance 8 ft (2.5 m).

Nurseries

In addition to general nurseries offering shrubs and herbaceous plants, the following specialise in ground cover:

Axletree Nursery, Starvecrow Lane, Peasmarsh, near Rye, East Sussex

Dartington Hall Nurseries, Dartington Hall, near Totnes, Devon

Growing Carpets, The Old Farmhouse, Steeple Morden, near Royston, Herts

Morehavens, 28 Denham Lane, Gerrards Cross, Bucks (camomile)

Rock Farm Nursery, Gibbs Hill, Nettlestead, near Maidstone, Kent

Wingwell Nursery, Top St, Wing, near Oakham, Leics

Creeping Jenny, *Lysimachia nummularia*, develops into thick, shining green mats

Above: candytuft, *Iberis sempervirens*, is an old favourite in gardens
Below: the flowers of *Hosta rectifolia* 'Tall Boy' add to its attractions as
a foliage plant